By the same author

Victorian and Edwardian Middlesex from old photographs, Batsford, 1977

How Haringey Grew, Hornsey Historical Society, 1985

St Mary's Church, Hornsey, Friends of Hornsey Church Tower, 1990

Exhibition catalogues for the London Borough of Haringey:
Willingly to School ... to mark the centenary of the 1870 Education Act (1970)
Time Off ... leisure time activities in Haringey up to 1939 (1972)
Transport through Time ... local transport and communications (1981)

Articles, including

(with Douglas Moss) "A fifteenth century Middlesex terrier", LMAS *Transactions,* vol.25, 1974.

Cover Part of John Ogilby's Map of Middlesex, c.1677

Haringey Before Our Time

A Brief History

by

Ian Murray

Hornsey Historical Society

1993

ISBN 0 905794 09 5

Hornsey Historical Society

First Published 1993

© Copyright Ian Murray and Hornsey Historical Society

Typeset by Pennant Press in 10 point Times Roman
Printed and bound by J.G. Bryson (Printer) Ltd.
156-162 High Road, East Finchley, London N2 9AS

INTRODUCTION

The need for a short history of our borough has long been felt. Surprisingly perhaps, *Haringey Before our Time* is the first on the general market. It evolved out of the author's "Haringey in the Past" which was a duplicated booklet available from Borough libraries in the late 1980s. An earlier version was called "Haringey in History". Ian Murray was for many years Archivist to Haringey Libraries and was based at Bruce Castle Museum in Tottenham. We are grateful to the authorities for permission to publish his work.

Joan Schwitzer and Malcolm Stokes have revised the text, with the full agreement of the author, to meet new demands arising out of the local history requirements in the National Curriculum. The illustrations have been chosen partly with this readership in mind. Suggestions from other members of the Hornsey Historical Society publications committee, notably Ken Gay and Susan Hector, have been most helpful. Peter Curtis has overseen the design and production with his usual enthusiasm and efficiency.

J.S.   Hornsey, 1993.

List of Illustrations

The publishers would like to thank the following for their kind permission to allow their works to be reproduced:
Nos. 2, 3, 4 and 9 — Messrs. A & C Black; 5, 6, 10, 12, 15 and 16 — Bruce Castle Museum, Tottenham; 7, 13, 17 and 18 — Guildhall Library, City of London.

THE MIDDLESEX HUNDREDS
OF EDMONTON AND OSSULSTONE

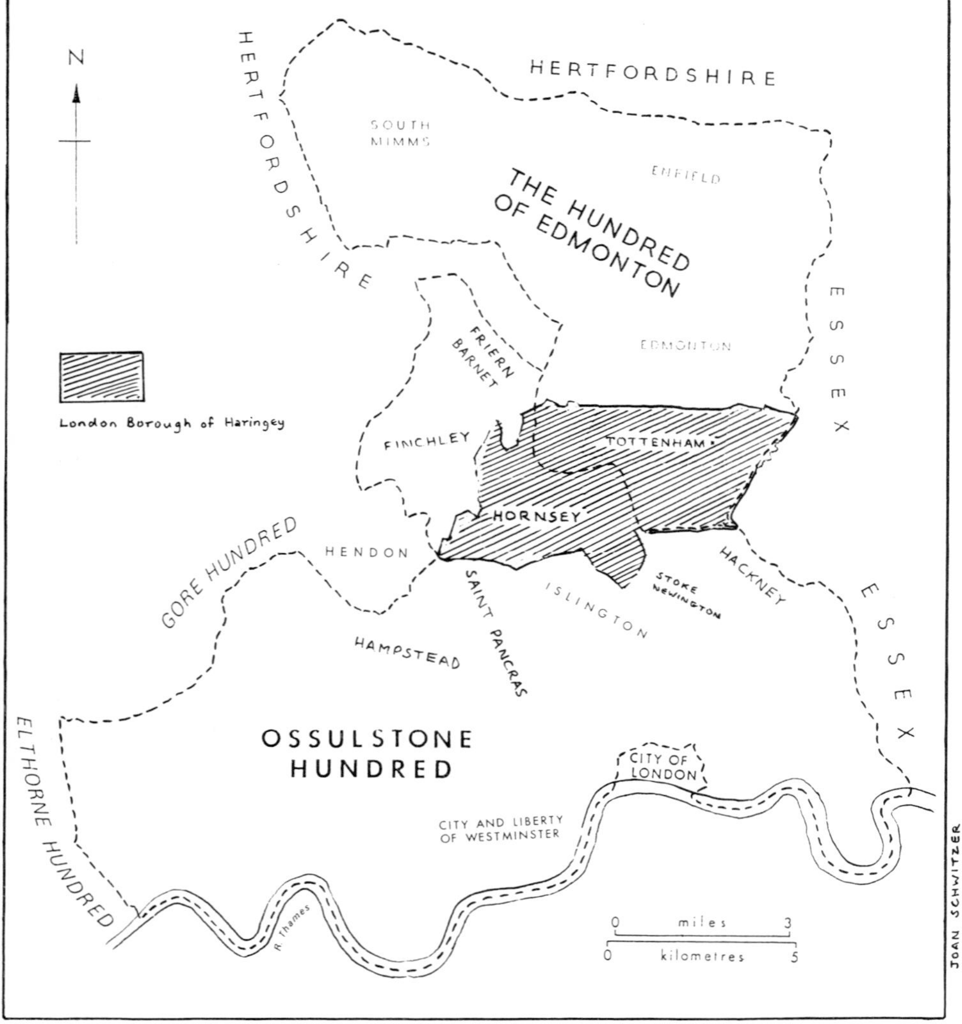

N

HERTFORDSHIRE

HERTFORDSHIRE

SOUTH
MIMMS

ENFIELD

THE HUNDRED
OF EDMONTON

EDMONTON

FRIERN
BARNET

FINCHLEY

TOTTENHAM

E
S
S
E
X

HORNSEY

London Borough of Haringey

GORE HUNDRED

HENDON

SAINT PANCRAS

ISLINGTON

STOKE
NEWINGTON

HACKNEY

E
S
S
E
X

HAMPSTEAD

OSSULSTONE
HUNDRED

CITY OF
LONDON

ELTHORNE HUNDRED

CITY AND LIBERTY
OF WESTMINSTER

R. Thames

| 0 | miles | 3 |
| 0 | kilometres | 5 |

JOAN SCHWITZER

The Hundred, a division of the Shire, was well established by the tenth century. Originally, it was probably an association of a hundred warriors and their families, later of around hundred settlements. The Hundred courts met every month to deal with local disputes and to maintain law and order. In Norman times they were gradually replaced by the Manor courts and by the Shire system operated mainly by Justices of the Peace.

Modern Haringey consists of the former boroughs of Hornsey, Wood Green and Tottenham which were amalgamated in 1965 under the London Government Act (1963). Tottenham and Hornsey had both been ancient manors formed almost certainly before the Norman Conquest, and they became parishes with established boundaries before 1300. Wood Green had been part of Tottenham Parish but had become a separate district in 1888, then a borough in 1933. Thus from a historical point of view Haringey is a recent creation and any account of it must be written in terms of three different areas, Hornsey, Tottenham and Wood Green. But they had much in common regarding growth and institutions, having a similar geographical character and experiencing a similar pattern of early settlement.

IN THE BEGINNING

From its eastern boundary, the River Lea, Haringey extends westwards some four miles or so into the high ground, known as the Northern Heights, which forms one side of the Lea and Thames valleys. Traces of prehistoric human and animal life in the form of flint implements and bones have been discovered, particularly along the Lea. Relics of Roman occupation are fairly extensive. Apart from a scattering of coin finds, excavations in Highgate Woods have revealed what was probably a small family pottery. For this local clay as well as timber for firing existed in abundance, and it seems to have been operated on a seasonal basis. There is a conserved kiln from this site in Bruce Castle Museum. An important Roman coin hoard now in the British Museum was discovered at Cranley Gardens on the south side of Muswell Hill in 1928.

The evidence suggests that a trackway existed in Romano-British times across what is now Hampstead Heath and Highgate connecting the two main roads from London to the north, Watling Street going to the north west of Britain and Ermine Street to the north east. Ermine Street, from London to Lincoln, seems to have mostly followed the line of the present Tottenham High Road, skirting the Lea marshes just above flood level. As yet no traces of Roman settlement have been found in this area, but dwellings have been excavated across the borough boundary in Edmonton, and it would seem surprising if there had been none in eastern Haringey.

In the fifth and sixth centuries, Saxon invaders founded permanent settlements where conditions were suitable. Haringey consists mostly of London clay with occasional patches of brick earth and gravel, and its then dense oak forests tended to discourage settlers. Along the banks of the River Lea, however, light alluvial soils allowed easier cultivation and there was a constant water supply. Here the village of Tottenham was founded, and further north Edmonton and Enfield. The names given by the Anglo-Saxons explain their origins. Tottenham means "the homestead of Tote" or perhaps "Tote's people".

Anglo-Saxon settlers clearing forest land

Gradually the forested areas to the west were also cleared and settled, as population pressure created fresh demand for agricultural land. The place names show the original nature of the landscape. Wood Green, formerly Wood Leigh, and Finchley were both 'leas', i.e. clearings in forest. The name of Hornsey signifies 'the hedge surrounding the settlement of Hering's people'. The original name was Haringseye, in various forms, which eventually shortened to Harnsey or Hornsey. The name of the modern borough is merely a revival of one of these medieval forms, as is Harringay, adopted for the new development along Green Lanes in the 1880s and 1890s.

In the epoch before the Norman Conquest, the county of Middlesex was established and divided into administrative areas called *Hundreds*. Hornsey was in Ossulstone Hundred and Tottenham in Edmonton Hundred. The importance of the hundred in local government declined as that of the manor grew. *Manors* were estates controlled by a landowner called a Lord of the Manor, many of whose tenants were obliged to perform labour services on his land. In return they were given land to cultivate for themselves and protection, but they were bound to the manor and were not able to leave without the lord's permission, at least not in the early period. The lord had the right to hold courts which recorded the transfer of land and dealt with petty crimes and nuisances. The manors of Tottenham and Hornsey were thus self-contained units of administration and forerunners of modern local government. The Tottenham court records survive from 1318 and give a detailed picture of life centuries ago. The Lord of the Manor of Hornsey was the Bishop of London; his records were kept at St. Paul's Cathedral and the early ones were probably destroyed in the 1666 Great Fire of London.

TOTTENHAM

Very little is known in detail about any part of Haringey from the era of the early settlements until the eleventh century. A few local glimpses are given by the Anglo-Saxon Chronicle, particularly over the struggle between Alfred the Great and the Danes. In 894, the Danes had taken their boats up the River Lea as far as the town of Ware; Alfred had the stream dammed and diverted so that the Danish vessels were stranded and had to be abandoned, forcing the crews to retreat overland. There is also a reference to a battle between Danes and Saxons under Edmond Ironside at 'Clayehangra'. This may possibly be near modern St. Ann's Road, which until comparatively recently was known as Hanger Lane.

Warfare devastated the area from time to time, but normally the main concern of the inhabitants of Tottenham is likely to have been the struggle to grow enough food for survival. The land under cultivation spread westwards as the forest was gradually cleared, and by 1619, the date of the first known map of Tottenham, all that remained of the woodland was west of Wood Green, where Alexandra Park is now.

The Danes invading by river

Medieval strip farming in the open fields

Tottenham is first mentioned in written records in Domesday Book (1086), when the Lord of the Manor was Waltheof, son of Gospatric, Earl of Northumberland. Both father and son are commemorated in local street names. The Domesday survey was commissioned by William the Conqueror, for taxation purposes, and provides invaluable information on land use and population. It shows that the Tottenham demesne land, i.e. land held by the lord himself and cultivated by his serfs or villeins, amounted to about 872 acres. The common pasture and arable land, shared by the tenants, totalled 1500 and 916 acres respectively. If we add road, meadows and woodland which supported 500 pigs, the total roughly equals the present area of Tottenham and Wood Green combined: 4642 acres. The population was recorded as consisting of 59 serfs, 4 slaves, two freemen, and a priest. It was only a few hundreds until the seventeenth century or even later.

Rural life was not all bliss. In 1381, at the time of the Peasants' Revolt, Tottenham seethed with unrest; tenants spoke out in court against the injustices of the Steward, and were heavily fined. One of the priests who spread news of the Revolt and co-ordinated local uprisings apparently came to Tottenham, but no major disturbances took place there.

By the sixteenth century tenants were free in practical terms. Money rents for land had everywhere replaced labour services. Restrictions on personal liberty, such as inability to leave the manor or to marry at will, had also disappeared. The economic basis of the manor too had changed. Subsistence farming had to a great extent been replaced by the production of crops for London, particularly hay. Much of the land had been bought by rich London merchants who tended to monopolise the market and to amalgamate smaller holdings as an investment.

London butchers bought land to graze livestock before sale at Smithfield, the cattle being purchased as far afield as the Midlands. Industry had made its mark too, with brick earth being used for the manufacture of bricks and tiles - first mentioned in 1427, when bricks sold at the equivalent of 25p the thousand. These brick earth deposits gave rise to the local clay industry which lasted into the twentieth century; South's potteries in White Hart Lane, making flower pots, lasted until 1961.

Local brick can be seen in the porch of All Hallows' Church and in the fabric of Bruce Castle nearby. Bruce Castle is recorded in 1254 as Tottenham's manor house and there are later references to a moat and drawbridge. It was probably built for a visit by Queen Elizabeth in 1568 and was again substantially altered in the 1680s by the Coleraine family, whose arms appear on the north side. The date and purpose of the red brick tower in front of the building has always been a mystery.

Bruce Castle, Tottenham's manor house, around 1700

The name Bruce Castle always arouses special interest, but it is somewhat misleading. The Bruce connection came about as follows. Judith, the wife of Waltheof, lord of the manor in 1086, had a daughter, Maud, who married David, King of the Scots. Thus the manor passed into the hands of the Scottish royal family. They retained it for nearly two centuries, and at the time of the revolt of the Scots, against the English Crown, part of the manor belonged to the rebel Robert the Bruce, who later became King of Scotland. He did not live at Bruce Castle, despite the name later attached to it. After the revolt, the lands of the Scottish kings in England were confiscated, including the Manor of Tottenham, and thereafter all Scottish connection with the area ceased. The name Bruce Castle probably came into existence in the eighteenth century, as a suitably romantic name for the building.

The medieval church of All Hallows' Tottenham

It was King David of Scotland who bestowed the Church of All Hallows, Tottenham's medieval church, on the Canons of Holy Trinity London as far back as 1134. To-day, much of the original building remains — the tower is fourteenth century — though it was much 'restored' in the nineteenth century by the architect William Butterfield. The church is an important link with the past, not only because of its age and the monuments within (which portray long vanished landowners such as the Candelers and the Barkhams) but because it was for centuries the seat of local government.

The *Vestry* of the church, meaning an assembly of parishioners, gradually replaced the manorial court in the administration of local affairs. The Vestry in practice was restricted to those with the leisure to attend but it kept the church in good repair, and arranged about such matters as proper seating. The Vestry also attended to general local matters such as repairing the roads and giving food or money to the poor. We find that quite generous benefits were given to local paupers but that paupers from other parishes were actively discouraged. Expedients were used such as paying pregnant women to go away, lest their offspring should become a charge on the rates. A function of the church from the sixteenth century onwards much appreciated to-day, was the compiling of registers of baptisms, marriages and burials; they help people trace their family history. An unusual baptism in 1611 was that of Walter Anburey, son of Nosser, born in Dongola which is now the Sudan; Nosser may have been a slave before finding his way to this country.

Very near Tottenham Green, at a high point in the High Road, stands Tottenham High Cross. One of the wealthier inhabitants of Tottenham, Dean Wood, replaced the old and rotting High Cross with a cross in brick in 1809. This is substantially the one that exists to-day. The manor court rolls (the parchment records) mention the theft of the cross's lead roof, which probably hastened the need for repair. The origin and purpose of the cross is unknown. It could have been a market cross but there is no evidence of Tottenham ever having had a chartered market. It may have been set up as a landmark to guide travellers, or have been a simple wayside crucifix. One thing is certain; it is not an 'Eleanor' cross, as has so often been stated.

Another local landmark used to be the Seven Sisters. These were seven elm trees which stood in Page Green at the south of Tottenham. They are mentioned by William Bedwell in his *History of Tottenham,* published in 1631, as being long established even then. Writers have attempted to link them with a pagan site in pre-Roman times, but, like so many curiosities in Tottenham, their origin is shrouded in mystery. The name is perpetuated in Seven Sisters Road, built to link Tottenham with the West End of London in the 1830s, which starts from Page Green.

By the eighteenth century Tottenham had become a fashionable urban village with its farms growing crops for the London market. But it remained separate from the metropolis until after the mid nineteenth century. Being on the main turnpike road to the north, it received an almost constant flow of traffic. This accounts for the large number of historic public houses along the High Road. One of these was the George and Vulture on the east side of the High Road just south of Bruce Grove junction. It was owned during the late sixteenth century by Balthazar Sanchez, a confectioner and immigrant to this country from Jerez in Spain. He became sweet maker to King Philip and introduced the art of confectionery to England. A convert to Protestantism, he was a local benefactor who founded the Sanchez almshouses "for the love and affection that I bear for the poor aged people, widows and widowers, inhabitants of the Parish of Tottenham." The almshouses, situated in the High Road, to the north of the George and Vulture, survived the first world war. Another historic inn which still survives, is the Swan, a favourite resort of Isaac Walton, the famous angler, after fishing trips in the River Lea. It stands on the corner of Philip Lane just north of Tottenham Green.

Tottenham Mills on the River Lea

The local water mill on the Lea ground Tottenham's corn for centuries but was used industrially later. It manufactured gunpowder for a brief period in the 1650s until local objections put an end to that particular activity. It is shown as a paper mill in Rocque's map of 1745, and was grinding oil seed at the time of a fire in 1850 after which it was never rebuilt.

Bruce Castle has had a varied history too. Much of the land attached to the house was sold in 1789 and the building eventually came into the possession of the Hill family who kept a school there from 1826 until 1877. The school was run on very advanced lines for that period and attracted a high proportion of pupils from overseas, particularly from the newly independent countries of South America. But the most famous member of the family is undoubtedly Sir Rowland Hill, who left the school in 1833 to enter government service. He is best known for his Post Office reforms, in particular the introduction of nation-wide prepaid postage in 1840, using stamps. This was the original postage stamp, known as the "penny black". It replaced the system whereby the charge for postage depended on the weight of the letter and the distance it was carried, and moreover was paid by the recipient.

Tottenham's population increased as new houses and villas were built along the High Road and along the country lanes leading to it. These included Philip Lane, West Green Road, and St. Ann's Road, and, notably, Northumberland Park, a high class development named after a Tottenham resident who became Duke of Northumberland. The area also began to change in character as immigrants from other parts of Great Britain and from overseas moved in. St. Francis de Sales Church, for example, had its origins in a Catholic chapel in Queen Street opened in the 1790s above a beer house, for emigrés from France after the 1789 Revolution. The chapel had been helped by John Eardley Wilmot of Bruce Castle. In 1826 it moved to Chapel Place, White Hart Lane, under Reverend M. Le Tellier, a French priest. This Catholic congregation was joined by Irish immigrants, whose number increased greatly during the nineteenth century, particularly at harvest time. The church was rebuilt in Brereton Road in the 1880s and the building can still be seen off White Hart Lane as part of an industrial estate.

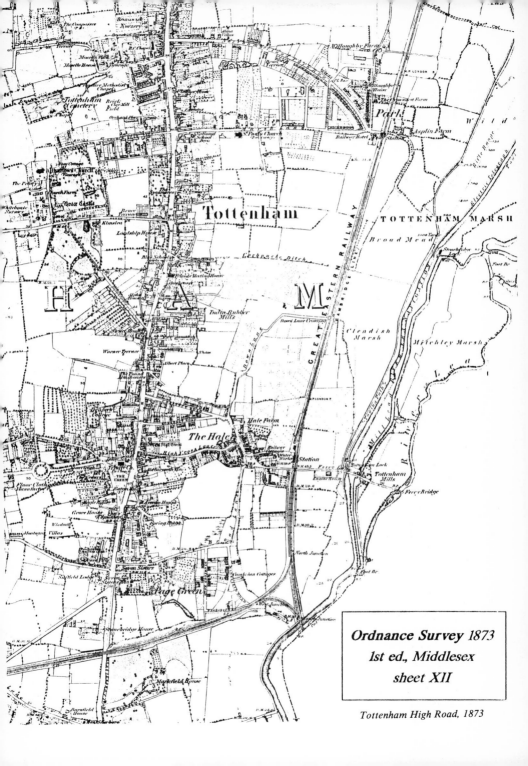

Ordnance Survey *1873*
1st ed., Middlesex
sheet XII

Tottenham High Road, 1873

A somewhat unexpected resident of West Green Road was Pepple, who had become King of Bonny in West Africa in 1839. He had complaints against the British, who had promised him compensation for loss of income after the abolition of the slave trade in 1833; the promise was later withdrawn on the grounds that he was not a deserving case. In retaliation he stopped all other trade. Pepple became such a nuisance to the British that in 1853 he was deposed; he was invited to live in Tottenham by a group of Quakers, and his two maids, Mary and Jane, attended the local Lancasterian school. Pepple returned to Bonny in 1861 and died five years later.

The Tottenham area, being near to London, and on a main road, had long been a fashionable one. Many large houses with spacious grounds belonged to London merchants. They were often involved in foreign trade; Reynardson's house, for example, on the north side of Tottenham Green, was owned in the seventeenth century by Sir Abraham Reynardson, Lord Mayor of London in 1649 and a Governor of the East India Company. Later, many of the Georgian houses in Bruce Grove were owned by Tottenham's Quaker community, among them the parliamentarian W.E. Forster, who introduced universal primary education to England in 1870, and the scientist Luke Howard who invented the modern classification of the clouds. An interesting residence, now demolished, was Markfield, east of the High Road in south Tottenham; the owner was William Hobson, an extremely wealthy early nineteenth century builder and contractor responsible for building Martello towers and also part of the London docks. He and his wife had a family of thirteen daughters and three sons, and were visited in 1806 by the artist John Constable, who sketched the girls and probably did his painting of All Hallows church (now in America) on that occasion as well.

In the nineteenth century change came rapidly. A silk factory was established in 1815, to be followed by a crepe factory in 1833 and a rubber works in 1837. Tottenham finally lost its air of exclusiveness after the opening of the Enfield to Liverpool Street railway in 1872. The Eastern Counties line had passed through the Lea Valley from 1840 but had failed to stimulate local housing development. The crucial difference was that the Enfield line offered cheap workmen's fares, and had stations at Seven Sisters, Bruce Grove and White Hart Lane. Thus the growth of Tottenham as a working class suburb was encouraged. The population rose dramatically, from 9121 in 1851 to 71,343 in 1891. It was 157,772 in 1931 — the highest point ever reached. For a while Tottenham was one of the four fastest growing districts in the country, with a large Jewish and east European community concentrated round the Hale. After 1900, industry started to move into the cheaper land by the Lea, with firms such as Gestetners, Harris Lebus and John Dickinson involved. In the 1920s, the London County Council built the White Hart Lane Estate and the Urban District of Tottenham lost its remaining farmland. When Tottenham became a borough in 1934, it had assumed the form we know today.

WOOD GREEN

Wood Green was part of the Parish of Tottenham until it became a separate local authority in 1888. (This followed a petition from residents who objected to the dominance of Tottenham.) As the name suggests, Wood Green originated as a green or clearing in the forest. Early Anglo-Saxon settlement throughout the area seems to have been based on a series of clearings — Tottenham Green, West Green, Chapman's Green, Duckett's Green, Wood Green — joined by trackways which formed the later road pattern. In 1619, according to a survey of the parish made that year, Wood Green consisted of a cluster of about ten houses backed by Tottenham Wood.

A deer hunt in Norman times, when hunting became the privilege of the king and nobility

The woodland was a source of fuel and timber for local inhabitants and was also used for hunting by the King and his court. James I came frequently from London and from his nearby estate of Theobalds for this purpose. Tottenham Wood was also at one time the hiding place of two of the priests who attempted to restore the Catholic religion to Britain after the Reformation. Records tell us that John Brushford and John Todd entered the country from the Netherlands and hired a room in a cottage "in the woode by Totnam Highcrosse" for six or seven months in order to escape notice; for food they sent a poor man into London.

A major new geographical feature after 1609 was the New River, financed by Sir Hugh Myddelton to bring fresh drinking water from the Amwell springs in Hertfordshire to London. This man-made river as originally dug, wound its way through Wood Green and Hornsey, hugging the 100 foot contour, and was a great engineering feat. In 1858 it was straightened and partially culverted, passing under much of Wood Green in a tunnel.

Another noticeable feature is Duckett's Common adjacent to Turnpike Lane Underground Station (built in 1932). This is the only piece of open land that survives from Duckett's Manor which lay partly in Tottenham and partly in

Hornsey. The manor first appears in history in a grant to Laurence Duket of London in the thirteenth century. An estate of 400 acres, it had a moated manor house which stood near present day Wood Green High Road (once part of Green Lanes) approximately where Lymington Avenue is now. Owners included Sir John de Stannford, Lord Chief Justice to Edward III. In the fifteenth century, it passed to the Priory of St. Bartholomew Smithfield, but when the priory was dissolved by Henry VIII its property was seized and sold off. As late as 1840 the estate was still producing beef cattle which were driven down the still green Green Lanes to Smithfield Market. It was finally disposed of as building land in the 1870s, with Noel Park estate built over part of it in the 1880s and 90s.

The small size of Wood Green is shown by the 1801 Census which records a population of only 100. The hamlet had a smithy and an inn, the Nag's Head, popular with anglers on the New River, which then ran above ground nearby. By 1844 numbers had risen to 400 and the need for a local church was recognised by the building of a chapel-of-ease, later to become St. Michael's Church. This saved churchgoers the walk through the fields to the parish church of All Hallows at Tottenham.

A gazeteer of 1866 remarks of the district:

> It is a ward and chapelry of Tottenham Parish. The ward lies on the Great Northern Railway, six miles north of St. Paul's, London. It has a post office under Tottenham and a railway station. Population of ward – 3154 (1861). Houses – 565. The Royal Masonic School for Boys, a very fine building, here. The Printers' and Fishmongers' Almshouses are here, the latter an imposing edifice in the florid Tudor style.

The countryside around London was favoured for institutions of this kind. The Royal Masonic School buildings survive as Woodall House (where the Crown Court is) in Lordship Lane. The Printers' and Fishmongers' Almshouses have both disappeared, Printers' being replaced by the telephone exchange on Jolly Butchers Hill and Fishmongers' by the Haringey Civic Centre. The increase in population since the 1860s (400 to 3154) is striking. The same 1866 gazeteer dismisses Bounds Green as merely

> a locality in Middlesex adjacent to the New River and the Great Northern Railway. It has a Post Office under Colney Hatch.

The area was indeed still rural in the 1860s, but the development of Wood Green was already under way. The triangle between Green Lanes and Bounds Green Road had begun to be built up, a tobacco factory and gas works existed near the railway line, and Caxton and Mayes Roads had been laid out.

To the north there was open country until the few scattered cottages at Palmers Green were reached. The picture had not completely altered by the 1920s for open country remained out towards Bounds Green and Palmers

Green. In fact, in 1920 one could have walked from Wood Green northwards past Bowes Park and on to Enfield Chase and into Hertfordshire without traversing another built up area.

It was the growth of public transport — train and tram — that stimulated the development of Wood Green in the second half of the nineteenth century. In 1859 a station was built amid the fields for the Great Northern Railway line from King's Cross. The Rhodes family, the owners of Tottenham Wood Farm, had offered land for the station first in the hope of being able to transport milk from the farm more quickly to London and later to encourage residential development. The results were probably greater than foreseen. As Wood Green became built up, the station was enlarged. An additional line, the Palace Gates Railway, was constructed by the Great Eastern with cheap fares for workmen. Opened in 1878, it came from East London and the City through Seven Sisters and Noel Park and terminated near the existing Wood Green station. Both stations were used by visitors to Alexandra Palace. After a decline in traffic and closure during the two World Wars, however, the Palace Gates branch line has been closed and dismantled, but the main line through Wood Green, now electrified, is busier than ever.

For a short period in the 1880s Wood Green High Road was served by steam trams but because of the smoke they emitted and their consequent unpopularity they were withdrawn from service, after a public petition. Horse trams were substituted — until 1904 when electric trams arrived. In that year Wood Green was connected for the first time to Tottenham by public transport, and Lordship Lane, winding through fields, lost some of its charm.

Fishmongers' Almshouses, built in 1849 where the Civic Centre is now

Perhaps the most prominent feature of Wood Green is Alexandra Palace, originally opened in 1873, and served by a branch railway from Highgate. It was intended to be a counterpart to the Crystal Palace in South London as an

19

educational and recreational centre for North Londoners. The scheme had been promoted as early as 1858, but financial problems caused delay, although the park was opened in 1863 and was named after Princess Alexandra, who married the Prince of Wales that year. A racetrack was laid out and opened in 1868. The first palace was destroyed by fire only a fortnight after opening and the building which replaced it in 1875 suffered the same fate in 1980. The palace is important in the history of communications because the first public regular television transmissions in the world were started here by the BBC in 1936.

Tottenham Wood Farm, 1873, with the site for Alexandra Palace shown

O.S. 1873, Middlesex sheet XII

The obelisk commemorating Catherine Smithies

In the north of Wood Green, on the way to Palmers Green, Woodside House stands in its grounds on the east side of the High Road. Now an old people's welfare centre, it used to be Wood Green's town hall. Originally it was a private house known as Earlham Grove and belonged to Mrs Catherine Smithies; she was the founder of the Band of Mercy which encouraged children to be kind to animals, in the days when most vehicles were horse-drawn. A memorial to her was put up by her son — an obelisk which now stands in Trinity Gardens. (Until 1904 it stood in the middle of Bounds Green Road.) In 1958 Wood Green built a new town hall on the site of the Fishmongers' Almshouses near St. Michael's Church, and (as noted earlier) this became Haringey's civic centre.

As London suburbs, Wood Green and Tottenham differed greatly in social composition and character. This was partly because the Great Northern Railway serving Wood Green did not offer cheap fares at first. Moreover much of Wood Green, near the station, is hilly, thus more expensive to develop and therefore occupied by those who could afford higher property prices as well as higher fares to the City. It has more open space and included Muswell Hill Golf Course, one of the oldest in North London, as well as Alexandra Park. Cheaper developments tended to be situated in the flatter eastern side of Wood Green, e.g. Noel Park Estate which was started by the Artisans' & General Labourers' Dwelling Company in 1882 to provide good working class housing at reasonable rents. Noel Park Station served this estate. A guide book to the district published in 1894 is typical of the contemporary attitude to Wood Green:

> *This pleasant suburb boasts many handsome villa residences occupied by a better class than those who live in Tottenham proper.*

21

There has never been much industry in Wood Green. Barratt's sweet factory in Mayes Road, now closed, was exceptional. The area has always been remarkable for the high proportion of 'white collar' workers. An LCC survey of Hornsey and Wood Green in 1931 showed that about 250 out of every thousand of the employed inhabitants were clerks. Many of these worked outside the district, and this situation was reinforced when the Piccadilly Line was extended north from Finsbury Park; by 1932 stations had been opened at Wood Green, Turnpike Lane and Bounds Green. The modern development of Wood Green High Road as a major shopping centre owes much to the prevailing favourable conditions as regards public transport.

HORNSEY

There is no direct reference to Hornsey in the Domesday survey as it formed part of the Lordship of Stepney which was given a consolidated entry in the Domesday Book. Hornsey is first mentioned by name in historical records as late as 1281 when it was claimed that the manor belonged to the Bishop of London "since time immemorial" — meaning before the Conquest. In the medieval period the district was heavily forested, and the bishops maintained a deer park and hunting lodge in Highgate. This lodge, which was apparently abandoned in the late fifteenth century, stood in what is now Highgate Golf Course; the park covered the area from the significantly named Gatehouse Inn at the top of Highgate High Street to the Spaniards Inn by Hampstead Heath.

In comparison with Tottenham, Hornsey was slow to develop, with a population of well under a thousand as late as 1674 (when the Hearth Tax returns allow a reasonably accurate estimate). Previously, in the Middle Ages, embryonic settlements in the woods and fields began to develop; they grew with time and finally merged in the late nineteenth century when the district became fully urbanised. The sites of the original settlements are still at the heart of recognisable neighbourhoods; these are: the main village along Hornsey High Street and around the church tower; Highgate — which has a distinct history of its own as a small country town; and the hamlets of Crouch End, Muswell Hill and Stroud Green.

Until the end of the fourteenth century, the main road to the north passed through Hornsey; from Holloway to Crouch Hill, along Park Road, over Muswell Hill, and so to Whetstone and Barnet. In wet weather it became impassable in places, and the route was gradually abandoned for one up Highgate Hill. The newer route went through the bishop of London's park, where tolls were collected, and across Finchley Common to Whetstone. This alternative was not without drawbacks, and the steepness of Highgate Hill eventually gave rise to the Archway Road bypass. The Archway was built in 1813 to carry Hornsey Lane over the cutting; the original plan was for a tunnel through the hill, but it collapsed in the course of construction.

Archway Road seen from the Archway Tavern, 1830

Like the rest of Haringey, Hornsey owes its development as a London suburb to the railways. The whole district is now laced with abandoned tracks. By 1850, Hornsey village was served by the Great Northern, although the prospect of a railway through the parish had been greeted with alarm by the local landowners who thought it would destroy the peace of the neighbourhood and reduce land values. From 1867, Crouch End had a station, which led to a great increase in house building; this line, from Finsbury Park to Highgate, is now Haringey's Parkland Walk. The population of Hornsey more than tripled between 1871 and 1891 — from 19,387 to 61,697 — and, as in Wood Green, development was mostly middle class. In the process big houses and estates which had been a feature of the district were bought up by land companies for suburban housing. The Harringay House estate between Green Lanes and Wightman Road, now known locally as "the ladder", and the Crouch Hall and Topsfield estates in Crouch End fall into this category.

Hornsey Village

The ancient nucleus of Hornsey round the parish church of St. Mary never developed into a major centre of activity, being overshadowed by Highgate in both numbers of population and in social status. Little of national importance seems to have disturbed the rural peace. But nearby, in Hornsey Great Park, a notable event occurred in 1483 after Richard of Gloucester, later Richard III, had intercepted at Stoney Stratford the young prince who was about to become King Edward V. They were met by the Lord Mayor and Corporation of London with five hundred men, and a royal procession to the City was formed with Richard in the guise of 'Protector'.

The church of St. Mary no longer exists apart from its medieval tower, and its history is a little complicated. The first mention of a church is in 1291 when it was assessed for papal taxation; a priest is referred to in 1303. The building lasted until 1832 when it was pulled down and replaced by a larger one which however retained the old tower. (This was completed by 1500; but there seems to be no

The Three Compasses tea garden. By 1860 the course of the river had been diverted and this section was culverted underground.

truth in the legend that it was built of stone from the bishop's hunting lodge.) The second church of 1832 came to be considered inadequate for Hornsey's increasing population, so yet a third was built, a little to the east on the site of the present St. Mary's Infants School, in 1888. The situation was that two churches, one disused except for bell ringing, stood side by side. Both have now gone and the ecclesiastical parish of St. Mary Hornsey is combined with that of St. George, Cranley Gardens.

The village, clustering round the church, was attractively situated. From 1609 the new River wound its way through it, crossing the High Street twice. In later years it drew many anglers, the Three Compasses with its tea garden on the river bank being a favourite place of refreshment. Broad and leafy Priory Road led from the High Street to the foot of Muswell Hill passing the mansion from which it took its name, The Priory, rebuilt in the 1820s. The last occupant of the house was a wine merchant, H.R. Williams, the first chairman of the Hornsey School Board which administered local state education after 1875; of him more anon. Nearby stood the village pound where stray sheep and cattle were kept until reclaimed by their owners. The charm of the place prompted the editor of an 1835 directory to write:

> *The neighbourhood is perhaps one of the most agreeable in the districts round London and is inhabited by persons of the first respectability.*

Crouch End

Crouch End consisted in the Middle Ages of two sub-manors of the Manor of Hornsey, Topsfield and Farnefields. Topsfield passed from the Bishop of London into the hands of Stephen Maynard in the fourteenth century. His name is perpetuated in a public house, the Maynard Arms, in Park Road — formerly called Maynard Street. Farnefields extended from Tottenham Lane up the hill to modern Mountview Road; the name survives in Ferme Park Road. At the junction of Maynard Street and Tottenham Lane, a wooden cross stood, and from this the name Crouch (or Crux i.e. Cross) End derives, as distinct from Church End further down Tottenham Lane and round Hornsey Church.

Until late in the nineteenth century a large house existed in the centre of Crouch End where Topsfield Parade is now, called Topsfield Hall. It was owned just before its demolition by Henry Weston Elder, a wealthy bristle merchant, after whom Weston Park and Elder Avenue were named. Another house sited between the present Coleridge Road and Crouch Hall Road, was the property of Sir Felix Booth of the gin-distilling family; it had a lake in the grounds known to locals as 'the lake of Gineva'. Crouch End's principal landmark, the clock tower, was erected in 1895 by public subscription to honour H.R. Williams of The Priory. His achievements included the preservation of Alexandra Park, Highgate Wood and Queen's Wood from developers. Now forgotten is the Crouch End Academy, a weather-boarded building formerly standing at what is now the corner of Crouch Hall Road and Park Road; it had been a school since the seventeenth century, and in the early nineteenth century became a boys's boarding establishment popular with officials of the East India Company. John Bewick, brother of the famous wood engraver Thomas Bewick, taught drawing there, commuting to his studio in London by pony.

Henry Reader Williams, local politician and campaigner, commemorated in his lifetime by a clock tower

This popular public house became part of Finsbury Park

Stroud Green

Stroud Green was formerly a marshy lane with a strip of common on either side and a very small population. A house call Stanestaple, occupied by the Steward of the Manor of Hornsey, existed there in the Middle Ages; it was later replaced by Stapleton Hall. Something about the district is revealed in the name of a former path over the hill from Stroud Green to Hornsey Village — Cut Throat Lane. Nearby was a piece of open country which had been a place of recreation for Londoners long before it was formally opened as Finsbury Park in 1869. Two pubs, Hornsey Wood Tavern by the woodland and Eel Pie House attracted large crowds on holidays; both were very near the New River, winding along through the fields.

Muswell Hill

Here again the Bishops of London shaped the course of local history. Around the well which gives Muswell Hill its name 64 acres of the manor of Hornsey were given to the nuns of Clerkenwell Priory in the twelfth century. They used the land for a dairy farm and maintained a chapel there. Water from the Mus (or "mossy") well was reputed to have curative properties and attracted pilgrims for many years until the priory was suppressed in 1540. The well survived until 1898, and a plaque on a house in Muswell Road marks the spot.

One of Muswell Hill's distinguished residents was Sir Julius Caesar, born in Tottenham in 1550. His remarkable name was bestowed on him by his father Cesar Adelmare, an Italian who became physician to Queen Elizabeth I. Sir Julius rose to high rank, becoming Master of the Rolls under James I. Mattisons, the property he owned on Muswell Hill, was later acquired by the Rowe family, prominent City traders in Africa and America. Another house on Muswell Hill, called The Grove, was occupied as a summer residence in the late eighteenth century by Topham Beauclerc, aristocrat, book collector, art connoisseur and amateur scientist. At Oxford, he had met Dr Johnson and the two were friends for the rest of Beauclerc's short life, which ended at the age of 41 from drug abuse and general dissipation. Dr Johnson was a frequent visitor to The Grove, and was an admirer of his friend's wife, Diana, a gifted painter whose portrait by Reynolds hangs in Kenwood.

Muswell Hill Common in the eighteenth century, with the Green Man at the top of the hill.

In the Middle Ages Muswell Hill was wooded and evidence of this is found in local pub names; one is the Green Man, first recorded as an alehouse in 1555. The Society of Woodmen of Hornsey, founded in 1750, practised archery and held meetings for many years. In medieval times the wooded seclusion of the district encouraged highway robbers who preyed upon travellers in Colney Hatch Lane and Finchley Common. Later, in safer times, Muswell Hill developed literary connections. Thomas Moore, the poet, author of the lyrics published as *Irish Melodies,* which included "The Last Rose of Summer", lived at the foot of Muswell Hill in 1817, and his daughter Barbara is buried in Hornsey churchyard. Frederick Harrison, a now almost forgotten Victorian philosopher and literary critic, wrote of Muswell Hill in his childhood,

> *We would wander there all day and meet no one but a carter or a milkmaid....*

The western part of Hornsey, being hilly, remained rural for longer than other parts, some of it until the 1920s. Muswell Hill had a railway station in 1873, but the line was frequently closed in response to the declining fortunes of Alexandra Palace, where it terminated, so that for prospective commuters the district was at a disadvantage. But development, once it had begun, was rapid: the whole of Muswell Hill was built over in twenty years after 1895. Most of it was carried out by the two building firms of Collins and Edmondson, with Edmondson laying out the Broadway shopping parades. The Rookfield Estate, covering the eastern lower slopes of Muswell Hill was completed by Collins early in the twentieth century, and is an example of a landscaped housing estate similar to its contemporary Hampstead Garden Suburb. Both were based on the model of Letchworth Garden City in Hertfordshire.

Highgate

Highgate is only partly in Haringey being divided by borough boundaries that were formerly parish lines of demarcation. These divisions suggest that Highgate was not an early Anglo-Saxon settlement. But by the sixteenth century it was well established and growing rapidly, favoured by the wealthy because of its hilltop position — considered good for health — and because of its situation on the Great North Road. As it was a regular stopping place on the route to the north, there were numerous inns and flourishing trades serving the needs of travellers.

Many people prominent in government or business have lived in Highgate. One not so well known resident was William Eaton, who sailed on the eighth voyage of the East India Company to Japan in 1611. He set up a trading post in Osaka but as there was insufficient trade the Company decided to abandon it in 1623. Eaton's Japanese wife stayed behind, but Eaton came home bringing his son with him to Highgate. By 1674, Highgate had more houses than in all the rest of Hornsey, a chapel-of-ease that was like a parish church, and a grammar school founded by Sir Roger Cholmeley in 1565 which survives today as

Highgate in 1827. A stage coach and a wagon are passing along the North Road.
Left, behind the trees the Gatehouse Inn

Highgate School. During the eighteenth century, the town maintained its fashionable character, and many buildings of that period and earlier remain to this day. On Highgate Hill, for example, on the elevated service road called The Bank, stand two fine seventeenth century houses known as Cromwell House and Ireton House. Since Highgate was in Parliamentary hands during the Civil War, legend connected these with Oliver Cromwell and his son-in-law, but it has long been established that the first belonged to the Sprignell family and that the second was probably named after a former Lord Mayor, Sir John Ireton.

Pond Square, as the name suggests, formerly contained ponds, possibly excavated by a hermit, William Philippe, in the fourteenth century, in the course of extracting gravel. This was used to repair the main road, which must have seemed like an act of charity to the poor of Highgate who acquired a convenient source of water.

The site of the Gate House Inn is of great antiquity though the present building dates only from 1905. It reminds us of the real meaning of the name Highgate, 'the gate in the hedge', i.e. the tall deer-proof hedge round the Bishop of London's hunting park. In the eighteenth century, the inn became famous for its "shilling ordinaries" — copius dinners that included two meat courses, a fowl and several pies. It was one of these hostelries that inflicted on new patrons the mock ceremony of "swearing on the horns". Practised in the 1840s (and recently revived), this was a device involving delay and consequent additional expenditure on drink. Coach passengers were assembled in a public room and made to swear nonsensical oaths while holding a pair of horns, before being allowed to continue their journey.

Highgate School and Chapel rebuilt for the tercentenary in 1865

Highgate has always attracted men and women connected with the arts and sciences. George Morland (1763-1804), the painter of country scenes, lived at the Bull in North Hill and is reputed to have produced some of his pictures there. The poet and philosopher Coleridge (1772-1834) lived in the centre of Highgate for eighteen years seeking a cure for opium addiction under the care of Dr Gillman.

A.E. Housman (1859-1936) wrote some of *The Shropshire Lad* while lodging in Byron Cottage in North Road. A house in Southwood Lane, as a plaque records, was the home of Mary Kingsley (1862-1900), neice of Charles Kingsley the author of *Westward Ho!*, who herself became a famous explorer of Africa.

Among the fine views of London from Highgate is that from Hornsey Lane above the Archway. William Howitt, Victorian journalist and historian, records the astonishment of Hans Christian Andersen who drove there at night and "saw the great world metropolis mapped out in fire below him". The present steel bridge was opened in 1900 by Louise, Duchess of Argyll, as a replacement for the original Archway. This was too narrow for a volume of traffic that was shortly to include electric trams.

The opening of Highgate Station in 1867 brought many new developments. But the semi-rural nature of the neighbourhood was preserved to a great extent. Highgate Woods were threatened with destruction by speculative builders towards the end of the Victorian era, but were saved for public enjoyment through the efforts of H.R. Williams and others. Queen's Wood was so called in honour of the Diamond Jubilee, but previously had the curious name of Churchyard Bottom. There was no churchyard near and one local tradition is that the name is derived from pits dug there in 1665 for victims of the plague. Unfortunately for this theory, the wood is referred to by that name in a manorial survey of 1649, sixteen years before the Great Plague of London. However there were many previous outbreaks of such epidemics, including the Black Death (1348). In 1603 a servant of the Earl of Shrewsbury wrote to his master telling him about over three thousand deaths from plague in London in each of the two previous weeks, adding:

> *In innes at Highgate, and other places within four or fyve miles of London, I may have choise of lodgings, but they are so dangerous by reason of generall infection yet I dare not to adventure in any of them.*

The area that is now Haringey has changed radically over the last century. The countryside has gone, and so has the old county of Middlesex of which it formed a part. Its appearance and the ways in which it is organised are all different, and so too are its inhabitants. Many of the parents or grandparents of today's residents came from overseas in the 1950s and 60s. But physical reminders of Haringey's long history survive everywhere.

Suggestions for further reading

The Borough of Hornsey 1903 - 1953 - a Jubilee publication,
Hornsey Borough Council, 1953

F E Butler & D Hoy, *Over the counter. A childhood view of shops in Tottenham and Wood Green between the Wars,* Edmonton Hundred Historical Society.
ISBN 0 902922 46 7.

Bridget Cherry, *Hornsey Church Tower. A brief history and guide,*
Friends of Hornsey Church Tower, 1990

Sylvia Collicott, *Connections. Haringey's Local, National and World Links,*
L.B. of Haringey, 1986. ISBN 0 903481 03 0.

Peter Curtis, *In Times Past. Wood Green and Tottenham with West Green and Harringay,*
Hornsey Historical Society, 1991. ISBN 0 905794 07 9.

Reg Davies, *Rails to the People's Palace,* Hornsey Historical Society, first published 1980, second ed. 1985. ISBN 0 905794 02 8.

David E D Freeman, *Looking at Muswell Hill,* privately printed, 1984

Ken Gay, *A walk around Muswell Hill,* Hornsey Historical Society, first ed. 1987, ISBN 0 905794 03 6. Revised ed. 1993

From Forest to Suburb. The Story of Hornsey Re-Told,
HHS, 1988. ISBN 0 905794 04 4

Palace on the Hill. A History of Alexandra Palace and Park,
HHS, 1992. ISBN 0 905794 08 7

Ken Gay & Dick Whetstone, *From Highgate to Hornsey. A Portrait in old Picture Postcards,* S B Publications, 1989. ISBN 1 870708 29 6

H G Hawkes, *Tottenham Shops. A Personal Memory,*
Edmonton Hundred Historical Society

Hornsey Historical Society Bulletins, first issued 1973. Annual *Bulletins* Nos. 22 and 25 onwards are in print. Nos. 30 to 33 (1989 - 1992) have separate titles;
ISSN 0955-8071. Articles deal with a great range of specialised topics.

Ian Murray - see list of publications on flyleaf

John Richardson, *Highgate. Its History since the fifteenth century,*
Historical Publications, 1983. ISBN 0 950365 6 4 5

Highgate Past, Historical Publications, 1989. ISBN 0 948667 02 8

Joan Schwitzer, *Highgate Village - Four Walks,*
Hornsey Historical Society, 1989. ISBN 0 905794 05 2

(ed.), *Lost Houses of Haringey,* Haringey Community Information with Hornsey Historical Society, 1986. ISBN 0 903481 02 2

Ben Travers, *The Book of Crouch End,* Barracuda Press, 1990.
ISBN 0 86023 465 7

Victoria County History of Middlesex, vol. 5, 1976, ISBN 0 19 722742 2; vol.6, 1980,
ISBN 0 19 722750 3. Oxford University Press for the University of London.